RISK MAN SIMP

A practical, step-by-step guide to identifying and addressing risks to your business.

Andy Osborne

Risk Management Simplified
A practical, step-by-step guide to identifying
and addressing risks to your business.
©Andy Osborne

ISBN: 978-1-906316-48-8

Published in 2010 by HotHive Books
www.thehothive.com

The right of Andy Osborne to be identified as the author of
this work has been asserted by him in accordance with the
Copyright, Designs and Patents Act 1988.

A CIP record of this book is available from the British Library.

Printed in the UK by TJ International, Padstow.

Over the years, my work with Chief Executives and Directors of businesses of all types has reinforced my belief that the effective management of risks is a fundamental aspect of exploiting business opportunities and managing a business. Indeed, it is absolutely essential if businesses are to succeed and thrive.

However, while effective risk management is important to businesses of all sizes and types, it has often been, and to a large extent still is, seen as the domain of very large organisations. But every business, whether it employs 5, 25 or 250 people should be actively managing its risks, and the principles of effective risk management apply whatever the size of the business.

There are a number of books available on the subject of risk management. Many of them are aimed at people who are already risk management specialists or who have a particular risk management related role. Others are very specific in terms of their subject matter, focusing, for instance, on financial or insurance-related risk, which, while extremely important, aren't the only types of risks that businesses face. Several are highly technical in content or are complex and difficult to understand. Some are just plain dull!

Most succeed in making the subject sound rather inaccessible to the average business manager, who, let's face it, probably has 1001 other things to think about besides risk management. Very few cover the subject of risk management as a whole. Even fewer tell the non-risk professional how to actually go about it, and fewer still do so in a way that's easy to understand and implement.

This book is different. Written in an informal, no-nonsense style that is easy to read and easy to understand, Andy Osborne's book brings the concepts of effective risk management to a wider audience than that traditionally served by the majority of risk management publications.

While its content will undoubtedly benefit small to medium enterprises (SMEs) it is just as applicable to larger businesses, not-for-profit or public sector organisations looking to implement an effective risk management programme.

I showed Andy's manuscript to some of the business owners and executives that I work with and the view was that it was excellent and would prove very valuable to CEOs, MDs and other business managers.

This is not a book full of theoretical musings. It is a highly practical "how to" guide which gives a simple, straightforward and thorough, process which, if followed, will make your business more resilient.

Richard Ward CCMI Dip IoD
Group Chairman
Vistage International (UK and Ireland) Ltd.

An acknowledged expert in the field of risk management and contingency planning, Andy Osborne has spent over 20 years helping businesses of all sizes, across a broad range of industry sectors, to understand and manage their risks effectively. He is a firm believer that the role of a consultant or adviser is to simplify apparently complex processes and present them in a way that is easy to understand, not the other way around.

Andy provides the following risk management consultancy services to clients, through his company, Acumen:

- Business risk assessment;

- IT risk assessment;

- Fire risk assessment, audit and evacuation planning;

- Health and safety risk assessment and audit;

- Training courses (including an introduction to risk management);

- Emergency planning;

- Business continuity management.

To contact Andy, call 01386 834455 or e-mail him at aosborne@acumen-bcp.co.uk.

Andy's first book *Practical Business Continuity Management* (ISBN 978-1-906316-01-3), a collection of hints, tips and good ideas for getting the best out of your business continuity management programme, was also published by The HotHive (formerly Word4Word).

Table of contents

## Chapter 1

In this chapter we consider:

- Why we should bother thinking about risks to our business;
- The benefits of effective business risk management;
- What we mean by risk;
- Some of the risks that our business might face;
- Balancing opportunities and threats;
- Some of the possible uses for risk management;
- A simple but effective risk management process.

"To be alive at all involves some risk."

Harold Macmillan, former British Prime Minister

Introduction

Risk is unavoidable. Like the proverbial death and taxes, it's one of the few things in life that's inevitable. All businesses[1], whatever their size and shape, whatever markets they operate in and whatever products or services they provide, are constantly faced with a multitude of risks, large and small. Indeed, as you are undoubtedly aware, businesses can only prosper through successful risk taking.

The trick is for a business to strike the correct balance between risk and potential reward; to maximise its upside risk and minimise its downside risk. To succeed we need to manage risk appropriately, not to try to eliminate or avoid it as, in any

[1] The term "business" is used throughout this book. However, it is used in the widest sense as the principles and techniques discussed are just as applicable to organisations (e.g. not for profit or public sector) that might not consider themselves to be businesses in the truest sense.

case, that simply isn't possible. It's therefore essential that we understand the major risks to our business operations to enable us to manage them to our advantage.

Some risks are so minor as to be insignificant, whereas others have the potential to seriously affect our business's continued well-being. So it's important to understand the likelihood and the potential consequences of our own particular risks, and to take sensible, cost-effective mitigation measures for the more significant ones.

This book will help you to do just that; leading you through the process in a straightforward, no-nonsense way. It will help you to identify and manage your risks in a number of areas, such as strategy, day-to-day business operations, financial control, capitalising on potential business opportunities, launching new products or services, expanding or changing the shape of your business and managing projects, to name but a few (see page 29 for more details). It will guide you through the various stages of assessing and mitigating your risks without blinding you with pseudo-science, techno-speak or jargon.

Many large corporations commit significant resources to the management of risk. Most small to medium enterprises (SMEs), however, are unlikely to be able to afford this luxury. And although the potential losses for the smaller business may be more modest than for the large national or multi-national corporation, the stakes can be far higher, as SME's don't typically have anything like the same level of resources (people, money, equipment or facilities) at their disposal. It's therefore essential that the risk management system that they employ is simple, straightforward and effective.

The aim of this book is to provide directors, managers or owners of businesses with just such a system – to strip away the non-essentials, to remove much of the academic, theoretical or bureaucratic "baggage" that comes with many risk management books (interesting though this may be to those with time for it!), to remove some of the complexity and to get back to basics. The end result is a very simple, but above all usable, process that can be applied to the real world that the vast majority of business managers inhabit.

The benefits of effective risk management

There are a number of distinct benefits to managing our risks effectively, including:

- Informed decision making;

- A more resilient business;

- Increased likelihood of successful risk taking (capitalising on opportunities);

- Protection of revenue, profits or market share;

- Protection of reputation/goodwill;

- Improved product or service quality and reliability;

- Protection of valuable assets;

- Increased likelihood of achieving strategic goals or objectives;

- Reduced costs and/or increased profits;

- Less failures and downtime;

- Competitive advantage;

- Fewer nasty surprises.

Many risks are seen as having purely negative consequences and for this reason it's not uncommon for those involved in risk management to take a pessimistic view of risk. But we shouldn't forget that many risks also have positive consequences. Effective risk management can help us to reduce the negative and increase the positive consequences of risk, thus helping our business to grow and flourish.

Risk management has a part to play in your decision making, whether it be with regard to business start-up, strategy, exploiting opportunities, managing your various projects or in your day-to-day business operations.

Risk management can help you to justify your decisions – to your management team, your employees, your business partners, investors, creditors or customers – and it should mean that you go into things with your eyes open; that you make informed decisions rather than just acting on a gut feeling or a hunch.

> *"While 'risk' is commonly regarded as negative, risk management is as much about exploiting potential opportunities as preventing potential problems."*

BS31100:2008 **Risk Management Code of Practice**, British Standards Institution

Hints and tips

The foresight saga...

Hindsight, as they say, is a wonderful thing. It allows us to be wise after the event. With the benefit of hindsight it's much easier to see something that now seems obvious. How often have you heard the phrase "it was an accident waiting to happen" after the accident has happened?

Effective risk management aims to make us wise before the event – to use foresight, rather than hindsight, to identify potential problems and prevent the accident, incident or disruption from occurring in the first place.

Hindsight may be said to be a wonderful thing, but in reality it's a bit pointless. If you can develop a culture of foresight rather than hindsight, it'll make your business much more resilient.

What is a risk?

Look in any dictionary and you'll find a definition of risk. Here's one:

risk *n the possibility of incurring misfortune or loss; hazard, **at risk**, vulnerable.*

Other definitions, of which there are many, include:

The combination of the probability of an event and its consequences;

The threat or possibility that an action or event will adversely or beneficially affect an organisation's ability to achieve its objectives;

The effect of uncertainty on objectives;

The science of good guessing.

What we're really talking about is a potential future problem – or, indeed, opportunity – or the potential future effect of a decision or an action that we take now. And every decision we make or action we take contains some element of risk.

Risks come about when the vulnerabilities in our systems, processes, facilities or resources are exploited by threats. Examples might include the burglar or hacker who exploits the vulnerabilities in our physical or IT security system, or a fire that starts due to an electrical fault and spreads because of weaknesses in our fire detection and suppression systems, errors made by inexperienced or insufficiently trained staff, or a whole host of other things (see page 17 for more examples of the risks that our businesses might face).

Risks can arise as a result of our own business's activities or as a result of external factors such as legislation, market forces, interest or exchange rate fluctuations, the activities of others or even the weather. They can be a product of the business environment, the natural environment, the political or economic climate or of human inadequacies, failings or errors.

The bottom line is that risk may impact on our ability to meet our business objectives or even threaten the business itself.

> *"It's likely that something unlikely will happen."*
>
> Aristotle

Me, a risk manager?

The good news is that every one of us is an intuitive risk manager!

Being in business may be risky, but life is a risky business and we're constantly faced with countless risks that we have to assess and make decisions about. Most of the time we don't even realise we're doing it – we just do it naturally. Which is just as well really, as if we had to stop and think about it we'd spend all of our time assessing risks and never actually get anything done.

For instance, every time we cross the road or drive our cars or play sport, or carry out many other day-to-day activities, we have to assess and manage risks, identifying and assessing the threats that we face and working out appropriate mitigation measures. But we do this almost subconsciously.

So, if we're all risk managers already, what's the point of this book? Well, the difference is that here we're more concerned with assessing and mitigating *business* risks. The process is pretty much the same as for our intuitive method, it's just that we probably have a bit more time to think about things. In business we really need a slightly more structured system than the instinctive approach, to enable us to identify and quantify our risks a bit better before we make our decisions.

When we evaluate risks to our business we need to have a clear and reasoned method of doing so. We may have to justify our thinking to others. We may need to persuade others to do something as a result. Perhaps more importantly, the potential downside if we get it wrong may be extremely serious – for ourselves, for our employees, for our customers, or for our business as a whole.

> *"There is a new appreciation of the wider scope of risks facing businesses requiring them to look at risk in a more structured way... A good risk management process is an essential part of being in business."*
>
> **Institute of Chartered Accountants in England and Wales**

"Stuff" happens

> *"Whatever can go wrong, will go wrong."*
>
> Murphy's Law

The following are examples, in no particular order, of some of the possible risks to businesses. It is by no means a definitive or exhaustive list – rather it's intended to give a flavour of the types of risks that businesses are faced with. We only have to read or watch the news, or think of our own experiences to realise that, unfortunately, these events do happen – in some cases all too frequently.

- ☐ Fire
- ☐ Flood
- ☐ Computer failure
- ☐ Failure to exploit opportunities
- ☐ Theft
- ☐ Poor sales
- ☐ Late payment by customers
- ☐ Supply chain failure
- ☐ Over-commitment
- ☐ Workplace accidents
- ☐ Equipment disruption/failure
- ☐ Loss/unavailability of key personnel
- ☐ Power failure
- ☐ Bad debts
- ☐ Fraud
- ☐ Sabotage
- ☐ Interest/exchange rate fluctuations
- ☐ Human error
- ☐ Breach of contract/contract disputes
- ☐ Data loss
- ☐ Increased costs
- ☐ Loss of a major customer
- ☐ Environmental damage

- ☐ Cash flow problems
- ☐ Industrial action/disputes
- ☐ Insufficient profits
- ☐ Storm damage
- ☐ Customer dissatisfaction
- ☐ Pollution/contamination
- ☐ Computer virus
- ☐ Faulty products
- ☐ Illness/disease
- ☐ Lack of working capital
- ☐ Breach of regulation/legislation
- ☐ Litigation
- ☐ Vandalism
- ☐ Industrial espionage
- ☐ Business lost to competition
- ☐ Denial of access
- ☐ Contaminated products/product tampering
- ☐ Fuel shortage
- ☐ Negative publicity
- ☐ Absenteeism
- ☐ Workplace violence
- ☐ Insolvency
- ☐ Hostile takeover

Unfortunately, the past isn't necessarily that useful or reliable in helping us to predict the future. Just because a particular risk hasn't yet come to fruition doesn't necessarily mean that the risk isn't there. On the other hand it doesn't mean that it's imminent. The thing about unexpected events is that, by definition, they're unexpected. The reality is that only we, as business managers, can decide whether a particular risk is acceptable to our business.

Some of the risks in the list on the previous page are largely beyond our control, because they are due to external forces, such as nature or changes to the political or economic environment. While that may be true, it's interesting to note that many of the risks listed are down to the actions of people, with very few "natural" events and relatively few external influences over which we have absolutely no control. It's a sad fact that when we introduce people into the equation things often go wrong. Because, people being people, they sometimes do unexpected, dangerous or even stupid things; they don't follow processes; they cut corners; they make mistakes.

However, in many ways this is good news. Clearly we normally have little or no influence over natural events, the political or economic climate or the legal or regulatory environment and can only really take steps to mitigate their effects (for instance we can't prevent severe weather from happening, although we can choose not to locate our business premises on a flood plain). However, in many cases, it is possible to do something to prevent or reduce the likelihood of the man-made risks occurring in the first place.

 Case study

A manufacturing company fell victim to an industrial sized version of the well-known tarmac scam, whereby someone in a fluorescent jacket knocks on your door, tells you that they have some tarmac left over from a job they've just finished, offers to patch up your driveway and, if you're naïve enough to agree, presents you with a large bill for a poor quality job.

The upshot for this company was that a huge amount of management time and attention was diverted into resolving the problem and they ended up paying out a small fortune in legal fees.

The root cause was the fact that procedures – in this case the purchasing procedure – were not adequately communicated and had not been adhered to.

Before you read on, why not take just a few moments to consider, and note below, which of the risks listed on page 17 might apply to your own business and which therefore warrant further investigation.

You'll notice that each of the risks listed has a check box next to it, so you can either put a tick against each applicable risk or note them here…

Later on in the book we'll look in more detail at these and any other risks that you identify along the way.

It couldn't happen to me... could it?

We might be tempted to think that it will never happen to us, particularly if we're one of the fortunate few who have never experienced anything particularly bad or disruptive in our business.

Unfortunately though, things do go horribly wrong from time to time. And the reality is that bad things don't just happen to other people. History is littered with the casualties (large and small businesses alike) of events that they thought couldn't possibly happen to them.

In reality, almost every business is likely to suffer some sort of disruptive or damaging event or situation during its lifetime. While the consequences of many of these events will, though painful, be manageable or at least survivable, for the unlucky or unprepared some of them will have the potential to seriously damage the business. These more serious events will range from the headline grabbing fires, floods and explosions, through to product and environmental contamination, fraud and theft, and to the less news-worthy but equally debilitating power or technology failures and supply chain or cash flow problems.

The statistics don't make particularly happy reading:

- There were over 11,600 commercial fires in the UK in 2006[2]. The average cost of a fire in a commercial building is estimated at £43,800.

- Loss of IT affected approximately 40% of businesses in the 12 months to January 2009.

- There are more than 1.6 million reported workplace-related injuries in the UK each year (only about 40% of major workplace accidents are actually reported).

- Some 25% of UK businesses were adversely affected by extreme weather conditions (including floods and high winds) in 2008. The figures for 2007

[2] The latest year for which figures were available at the time of publishing.

and 2006 were 29% and 28% respectively.

- The annual cost of crimes against UK businesses is around £12.6 billion (this figure has increased by 20% over the last 5 years), with 59% of businesses experiencing at least one incident of crime in the last 12 months.

- Fraud is widespread and on the increase and cost UK businesses over £705 million in the first 6 months of 2008. Most fraud is carried out by senior or long-serving employees, with management fraud accounting for 46% of the total.

- Work-related road traffic accidents are the single largest cause of occupational fatality in the UK, with over 1,000 deaths a year as a result. Company car drivers are almost 50% more likely to be involved in a crash than any other driver, even allowing for their higher mileage.

- There were over 17,000 UK business failures due to insolvency in 2007 and 16,591 in the first nine months of 2008. Estimates for 2009 are around 19,100.

- Staff absence costs the UK economy over £13 billion per year, with over 170 million days lost to absence (over 10% of which are thought to be non-genuine). The average cost of absence is just over 3% of payroll.

- The failure rate for new businesses is high, with as many as 50% failing in their first 2 years.

(Sources: BDO Stoy Hayward, British Chambers of Commerce, Chartered Management Institute, Confederation of British Industry, Department for Communities and Local Government, Department of Transport, Experian, Health & Safety Executive, Royal Society for the Prevention of Accidents.)

Putting some time and effort into managing our risks is a worthwhile investment and makes good business sense. Ultimately, effective risk management could be the difference between the survival and failure of the business.

> *"If there's a 50% chance of something going wrong, then 9 times out of 10 it will."*

Anon

Case study

A popular and successful town centre restaurant was flooded when the nearby river burst its banks during a sustained period of heavy rain. Drying and refurbishment work took many months, during which time the restaurant remained closed for the whole of that year's tourist season, normally the busiest (and most profitable) time of year.

The flood was described as a "100 year event", but 8 years later the same thing happened again – except that this time the flood water was deeper. With another season's profits lost, the owner decided not to re-open and moved to a new location to start his business up all over again.

The balanced view

Almost every business opportunity has a potential downside. But some of the risks that we take also have a potential upside – that's why we take them. Indeed, a business may consciously decide, as part of its strategy, to take a high level of risk because of the potential rewards.

We need to balance the opportunities (to make a profit, grow the business, move into new markets, launch new products and services, etc.) against the potential downsides (such as over commitment, the impact of interest or exchange rate fluctuations, inability to sell our wonderful product or service, inability to pay our staff, etc.).

It's not possible to create a completely risk-free environment. But what we can do is manage risk more effectively. We can identify risks, quantify them and, once we understand what we're up against, we can make informed, considered decisions regarding what (if anything) to do about them.

> *"Who bravely dares must sometimes risk a fall."*

Tom Bradley, Mayor of Los Angeles (1973-1993)

Risk management applications

Risk management has many uses. Some of the possible applications are shown in the diagram below.

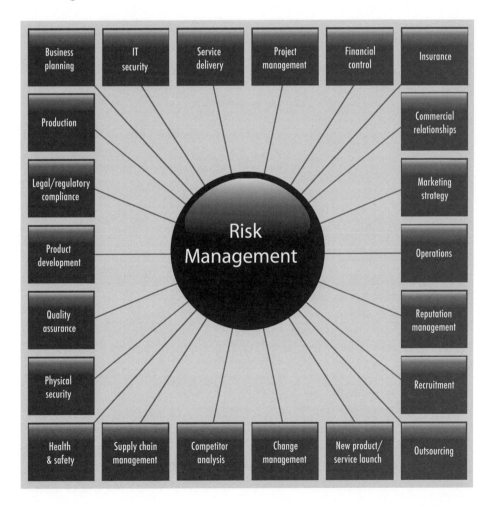

Risk management can be used to:

- Ensure the safety and well-being of employees, visitors, customers, etc;

- Make your business more resilient;

- Support your decision making process;

- Increase the likelihood of successfully exploiting opportunities;

- Perform "what if" assessments;

- Ensure legal or regulatory compliance;

- Protect your cash flow;

- Increase the likelihood of success in your projects;

- Support requests for action or expenditure;

- Improve the strategic and day-to-day management of your business;

- Improve operational processes and reduce failures and problems.

"Recent research indicates over 70% of programmes are late, over budget or ineffective. Organisations employing effective risk management have reduced this failure rate significantly and gained a significant competitive advantage."

Colin Wheeler, Technical Director, Istria

The risk management process

The risk management process introduced in this section is simple but effective. More to the point, it has been proven to work in businesses of all types and sizes. There are five very straightforward elements to the suggested process, which are shown in the diagram outlined below, and described in more detail in subsequent chapters:

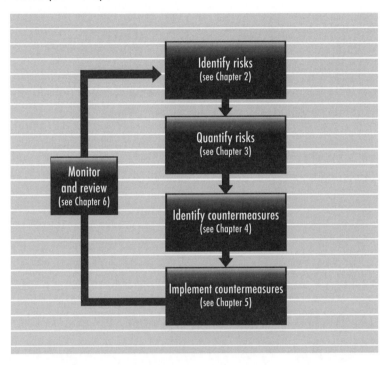

Before we can take any meaningful action to address our risks we need to know what we're up against. So we need to identify the risks that we face (more information on risk identification can be found in Chapter 2).

Then we need to quantify them in some way. Because what we're really interested in is the risks that we consider to be significant enough to do something about. So we need a way to sort the wheat from the chaff. We do this by assessing the likelihood of the risk occurring and the impact if it does. (Chapter 3 discusses likelihood and impact in more detail.)

Once we know which are the most serious we can start to deal with them, by identifying and implementing possible countermeasures, or mitigation measures – methods of removing, reducing, controlling or recovering from adverse events (Chapter 4 contains information relating to various risk response options).

Having determined which countermeasures we feel are sensible and cost effective and decided which ones we want to invest in, we can go ahead and implement them (see Chapter 5).

To complete the process we should monitor the effectiveness, or otherwise, of the controls we put in place (Chapter 6 suggests some considerations for this important, though often overlooked, stage).

The following five chapters explore each of the above elements in turn and provide useful information to help put them into practice.

"Only a person who risks is free. The pessimist complains about the wind; the optimist expects it to change and the realist adjusts the sails."

William Arthur Ward, American author

Follow up actions

This page is for you to note any key points or thoughts prompted by the content of the previous chapter and the follow-up actions you intend to take to help you manage risks in your business.

Section/page	Key points	Follow-up actions

Chapter 2 looks at the first stage in the risk management process – identifying risks.

In this chapter we consider:

- The types of risks that might apply to our business;
- Stage 1 of the risk management process – identifying risks;
- How to go about identifying specific risks to our business.

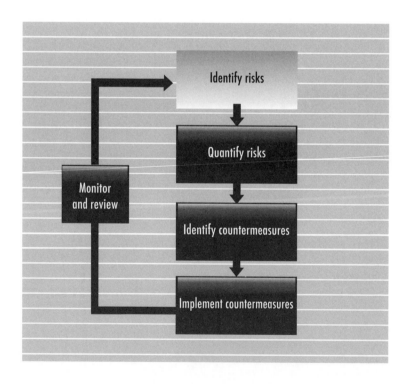

Identifying the risks – where do I start?

With all those possible risks out there, where on earth do we start? If we tried to identify every potential risk to our business we could make it a full time job. And for most of us this simply isn't an option. Therefore, we need to focus our efforts.

We need to concentrate on the risks to the most important parts of our business. These are likely to vary from business to business, but for many they might well include some of the following[3]:

Strategic risks, such as those associated with:
- Business planning and future direction;
- Achievement of strategic objectives;
- Business growth;
- New markets, products and services;
- Mergers, takeovers and alliances.

Operational risks, in areas such as:
- Supply of components or raw materials;
- Production;
- Distribution;
- Service delivery;
- Operator errors;
- Pollution, contamination and environmental damage.

Financial/commercial risks, for example to:
- Cash flow;
- Sales;
- Customer retention;
- Contracts.

[3] The risks in the above list are shown in the various categories (strategic, operational, financial, etc) purely for illustrative purposes and you may wish to categorise your own risks differently. For example, skills shortage, shown under personnel risks may also be categorised as an operational or project risk.

Regulatory/compliance risks, such as:

- Breach of regulation;
- Failure to meet legal or contractual requirements;
- Loss of operating licence;
- Legal action.

Health and safety risks, including:

- Workplace accidents;
- Serious injury or death;
- Litigation.

Personnel risks, for example:

- Loss or unavailability of key staff;
- Inadequate skills/skills shortage;
- Recruitment and employment;
- Workplace violence.

Technology risks, including:

- IT failure;
- Viruses, denial of service attacks, phishing, etc.;
- Plant/equipment failure;
- Data loss.

Project risks, such as:

- Failure to meet timescales;
- Increased cost/resource requirements;
- Failure to meet business requirements;
- Project failure.

An alternative way of looking at things is to think of the business's assets. These might include:

- Physical assets (premises, equipment, plant, tools, etc.);

- Monetary assets (cash in the bank or projected income);

- People (knowledge, skills and experience);

- Intellectual property (e.g. computer programs, designs, patents, copyrighted materials, etc.);

- Reputation and goodwill.

Once we've listed the assets, we can determine which are the most critical. We can do this by assessing the impact to the business of the loss of any of our assets, or our inability to perform a particular function. In this way we can focus on the risks to the most critical areas of our business.

It may also be helpful to group the assets (e.g. by location or function or product/service), so we can assess the threats to each group of assets as well as individually.

> *"You don't need a parachute to sky-dive – you only need a parachute to sky-dive twice!"*
>
> Anon

A business supplying industry-related data to its customers recognised the need to move from paper-based to online provision and invested significantly in developing internet-based services. The online side of the business grew rapidly to account for over 50% of its revenues.

The complexity of the IT and telecommunications infrastructure supporting the new services meant that very few people understood in any detail how it all linked together. In fact, there was a huge dependency on one member of the IT department, to the extent that the poor chap was constantly called in out of hours and while on holiday to resolve technical problems.

If this wasn't a big enough risk it was compounded somewhat by another issue. The company had a small satellite office in a converted farm building in the middle of nowhere. Because of a spate of false alarms there, the police refused to attend site when the burglar alarm went off until someone from the company had been to check things out. The person who lived closest, and therefore the one who frequently got called out in the middle of the night to go to a remote location, in the dark, on his own, where there was a potentially dangerous situation, was, you've guessed it, the person on whom the operation of the online services depended.

Incredibly, these risks had not been considered until a risk assessment highlighted them and senior management decided that they really ought to take steps to mitigate them.

Identifying the risks – how do I go about it?

Having identified the most critical elements of our business, we can set about assessing the risks to them. The most effective way of doing this is by using the technique of "brainstorming"[4].

While it's possible to do this on your own, it's generally far more effective if several people are involved. Involving others gives a more objective view and helps to avoid the "wood for the trees" syndrome, where risks that are obvious to some people are either not noticed, or worse still, ignored by those closest to them.

[4] Readers who are not familiar with the process of brainstorming should refer to page 96.

Once the brainstorming team has been established, all that's needed is a couple of hours without interruptions and a flipchart with the following columns drawn on it:

#	Risk	Likelihood	Impact	Rating

During the brainstorming session, it's important to focus on identifying *risks*. That might sound obvious – this is a risk assessment after all! However, it's easy to get sidetracked into thinking about *issues* rather than risks. There's a subtle but important distinction here. An issue is something that exists already, perhaps a prevailing situation that gives rise to specific risks. For instance, poor morale in itself isn't a risk, but it might give rise to the risk of key staff leaving or poor quality work. To ensure we stay focused on identifying risks, it can be useful to complete the sentence "there is a risk that…" or "there is a risk of…" for each of the risks put forward.

It's also important to stress that we're not looking for solutions at this stage, just the possible risks. And we don't want to get bogged down in assessing likelihood and impacts or the relative importance of each at this stage – more on that later. When everyone is "brainstormed out" and has nothing more to add, that's the end of the first part of the process.

You should now have a list of risks that might look something like this:

#	Risk	Likelihood	Impact	Rating
Commercial:				
1	Risk 1			
2	Risk 2			
3	Risk 3			
Operational:				
4	Risk 4			
5	Risk 5			
6	Risk 6			
Financial:				
7	Risk 7			
8	Risk 8			
	Etc.			

Work sheet

Before you read on, why not take a few moments to consider the key risks to your business in the categories shown on page 29 and 30 and note them below. You might then consider arranging a risk assessment workshop to discuss these and other risks with your colleagues.

Ref	Category (e.g. strategic, operational, financial, etc.)	There is a risk that...

In the next chapter we'll look in more detail at the *likelihood* of these risks occurring and the *impact* if they do. This will help you to focus on the specific risks that you feel need further attention.

Hints and tips

Narrowing the focus...

Anyone who's ever been involved in a risk assessment workshop will know that once you get started you can identify a shed-load of risks. There are just so many of them out there.

But, while some risks are potentially extremely serious, there are many others that are somewhat less significant. And, let's face it, it's the significant risks that we need to focus on. So we need to sort the wheat from the chaff and avoid getting too bogged down in stuff that isn't overly important.

One way to do this is to focus the risk assessment on our essential or time-critical functions, processes or assets and to set a specific objective for the workshop, such as identifying risks to cash flow or the supply chain or to the continued operation of a critical process, facility or piece of equipment.

There is therefore the implication that we know what's essential or time-critical. And, if we haven't already done so, an excellent way of identifying these things is to do a business impact analysis[5]. But that's another story...

---

[5] A business impact analysis focuses (as the name suggests) on the *impacts* of the unavailability of business functions, processes or systems. It measures these impacts over time, identifying the point at which their unavailability would be intolerable and helping us to determine the timescales and relative priorities for recovery following a disruption. While a risk assessment typically considers impacts at a fairly high level (e.g. high, medium, low – see next chapter), the business impact analysis usually looks at them in much more detail and considers a whole range of financial and non-financial impacts over various timescales. The business impact analysis can help us to decide which countermeasures to invest in and is often the first stage in the process of developing a contingency, or business continuity, plan (see also page 60).

Follow-up actions

This page is for you to note any key points or thoughts prompted by the content of the previous chapter and the follow-up actions you intend to take to help you manage risks in your business.

Section/page	Key points	Follow-up actions

Chapter 3 looks at the second stage in the risk management process – quantifying risks.

In this chapter we consider:

- Stage 2 of the risk management process – quantifying risks;
- Quantifying our previously identified risks by assessing likelihood and impact;
- Possible impact types and definitions;
- Rating our risks using a simple risk matrix;
- Prioritising by identifying significant risks.

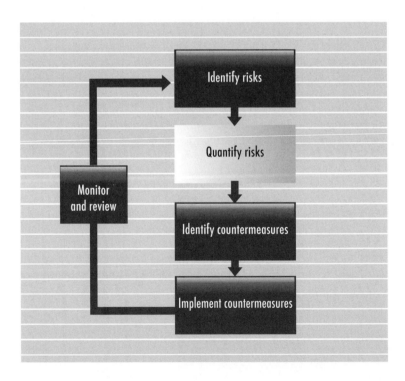

Quantifying our risks – likelihood and impact

If you've completed the brainstorming exercise outlined in the previous chapter the chances are you now have quite a long list of risks. Some of them may well be trivial, but some of them will be significant enough for you to want to do something about them – and it's those significant risks that we're most interested in. So we need to be able to quantify our risks in some way, so as to identify the significant ones. So how do we do this?

Our vulnerability to any particular risk is a combination of the **likelihood** of the risk materialising and the **impact** if it does. In other words, when assessing risks, we need to answer two simple questions:

1. How likely is it to happen? and
2. If it does happen, how much will it hurt?

When determining likelihood, we could take a scientific or analytical approach and seek out statistics from the emergency services, the environment agency, insurance companies, salvage companies or the multitude of other sources on the internet. Indeed, your average full-time risk manager in a large organisation will often use a lot of statistical analysis and historical information in determining the likelihood of particular risks occurring.

This is all very well if you have the time (and the inclination) to go to these lengths. However, there's a very real risk of over-complication and, more to the point, of spending an inordinate amount of time on it. In the vast majority of cases it's sufficient to determine whether the likelihood is high, medium or low. Alternatively we might use terms like unlikely, possible, probable and inevitable or a simple numerical scale, such as 1 to 3 or 1 to 4. For the purposes of outlining the process, in this book we'll use a 1 to 4 scale (see page 44).

When determining impact, we should bear in mind that impacts can be both financial and non-financial (although many of the non-financial impacts will ultimately result in some form of financial impact too), and can include:

Financial impacts

- Loss of revenue;

- Lost interest;

- Cash flow problems;

- Higher bank charges;

- Repair/replacement costs;

- Increased cost of working (overtime, additional staff, equipment, etc.);

- Consequential losses;

- Reduced credit rating;

- Fines or compensation payments;

- Regulatory penalties/fines;

- Impact on share price/reduced dividends.

Non-financial impacts

- Death or serious injury;

- Loss of credibility/goodwill;

- Negative publicity;

- Damage to reputation;

- Degradation of service to customers;

- Loss of production;

- Backlog of work;

- Pollution/contamination/ environmental damage;

- Legal action;

- Withdrawal of operating licence;

- Low morale.

While we need to consider which of the above types of impacts might be felt, for the purposes of the risk assessment it's probably sufficient to use a high, medium, low approach or a 1 to 3 or 1 to 4 scale, as we did with the likelihood rating. We'll use a 1 to 4 scale in this book (see page 43).

Hints and tips

What's in a name?...

Sometimes the terms "probability" or "frequency" and "consequences" or "severity" are used in place of likelihood and impact. It doesn't really matter which you use – whichever you feel more comfortable with.

You might just bear in mind, however, that the word "probability" can suggest a mathematical or scientific exactness that may not actually exist, which may be a good reason to avoid it.

In truth, risk management isn't an exact science and, while those obsessed with statistics might argue otherwise, the "probability" of unexpected events is largely unknown. This doesn't mean, however, that we shouldn't give it some thought!

Case study

An ex-employee of a market research company who had been sacked several months previously, broke into his former employer's offices at a weekend to steal laptop computers. Unfortunately, another member of staff who was also in the office recognised the burglar and was murdered during the ensuing argument.

The police sealed off the offices, which remained closed for several weeks while they carried out their investigation.

In addition to the trauma caused by the killing, the disruption to the business and negative publicity resulted in a huge loss of profits and considerable additional costs.

Assessing and rating our risks

We can either do this in splendid isolation, or better still as the second stage of the brainstorming process. It's useful to gain consensus, otherwise this can be a very subjective process unless, as previously discussed, we can afford the time to do a lot of statistical and historical analysis.

For each of the risks identified earlier, we now need to assign likelihood and impact ratings. Before we can do this though, we need to decide on the scale that we're going to use to rate our risks. As discussed previously, the two most popular approaches are to use words like "low", "medium" and "high" or a simple numbering system such as 1 to 3 or 1 to 4 (see "Risk Matrix" section on page 48). For the purposes of the example in this book, we'll use a 1 to 4 scale (where 1 is the lowest and 4 the highest).

Whichever scale we use, and whether we prefer words or numbers, it can help us to focus our minds and be a bit more objective if we think about what we mean by the lows, mediums and highs or the 1s, 2s, 3s and 4s.

By way of an example – and this is only an example as it will differ from business to business – the following table gives some possible ways to quantify the various levels of impact:

Impact ratings	Possible impact definitions	Impact examples
1 Low Insignificant Minimal	Inconvenience but no significant business impact.	Minor, short-term staff disruption; minor customer dissatisfaction; negligible financial impact.
2 Medium Moderate Unsustainable	Operational difficulty requiring significant time and/or resources to manage.	Minor injury; several customer complaints; significant staff disruption; non-trivial financial impact.
3 High Significant Major	High visibility, significant and/or sustained business issues.	Serious injury; significant customer dissatisfaction; damage to reputation; regulatory issues; serious staff disruption (e.g. effective operation of dept/project compromised); significant financial impact.
4 Severe Catastrophic	Threat to viability or survival of the business unit or the business.	Death; unacceptable customer impacts; serious damage to reputation; brand affected; operating licence revoked; high financial impact.

When thinking about likelihood, again we can use "low", "medium" and "high" or, if we prefer, numbers or even terms like "unlikely", "possible", "probable" or "inevitable". As with the impact ratings, in this example we'll use a 1 to 4 scale. The following table gives some possible ways to quantify the various levels of likelihood:

Likelihood ratings	Possible likelihood definitions
1 Low Unlikely	Not expected to occur or has not occurred in the past 20 years. Almost inconceivable, but cannot be ruled out entirely. Single figure percentage probability.
2 Medium Moderate Possible	Expected to occur or has occurred once in the past 10 years. Conceivable, but more likely not to happen than to happen. Less than 50:50 chance of occurring.
3 High Likely Probable	Expected to occur or has occurred several times in the past 10 years. More likely to happen than not to happen. Greater than 50:50 chance of occurring.
4 Almost certain Inevitable	Expected to occur or has occurred at least once a year. Difficult to conceive of it not happening. High (80+) percentage probability.

When considering likelihood, we might do some statistical analysis or even think in terms of percentages. A word of caution here though – statistically, a risk that occurs once or twice a year every year without fail can be shown to have an extremely low percentage probability, even though there's a cast iron certainty that it's going to happen again if we don't do something about it (the case study on page 50 gives a real life example of this). So it's not always helpful to try to be too logical or pseudo-scientific about assessing risk – common sense has an important role to play too.

Moreover, taking at face value statistical "evidence" that a particular risk is a 20, 50 or 100 year event (as seen in some insurance-related statistics) can be somewhat misleading. Just because a "20-year" event (such as a fire) hasn't happened for 19 years, it doesn't mean that one's imminent. And just because we experienced a "100-year" event (such as a major flood) last year, it doesn't mean that we're safe for another 99 years (see the case study on page 22 for a real-life example).

So while it's important to think about likelihood when assessing our risks, and whether we do so with or without the "benefit" of huge amounts of statistical or historical information, it's really just a guess, albeit an educated one. Indeed, for certain types of risk – in particular the low likelihood, high impact risks – a sensible approach may be to focus more on the impact than the likelihood (see also "Contingency planning" on page 60). This approach is borne out by the fact that many of the high profile, disastrous events of recent times had never happened before and were therefore inconceivable to many before the event – but it didn't stop them happening.

"We can't get much better at predicting. But we can get better at realising how bad we are at predicting."

Nassim Taleb, author

Two 2s are 4 – but not always...

It's fairly common practice in risk assessment to use a numerical scale (such as the 1 to 4 scale used in this book) when estimating likelihood and impact.

However, this approach comes with a health warning – it's important to realise that the numbers are really only there for convenience, and a level 4 likelihood isn't necessarily (in fact it almost certainly isn't) 4 times as likely as a level 1 or twice as likely as a level 2. Similarly, a level 4 impact isn't 4 times as bad as a level 1 or twice as bad as a level 2. Indeed, the increase in likelihood or impact between level 1 and level 4 could well be 20 or 50 or 100-fold or more (exponential).

The important thing here is where the risk falls on the risk matrix (see next section), as this will help us to consider which risks we ought to do something about and what we ought to do about them.

So, back to our brainstorming session. Using whatever scale we've decided to use – in this case 1 to 4 – we can now start to rate our risks. This is simply a matter of revisiting each identified risk, making a group judgement as to the likelihood and impact ratings for each and writing these on the flipchart. Our flip chart will now look something like this:

#	Risk	Likelihood	Impact	Rating
Commercial:				
1	Risk 1	1	2	
2	Risk 2	3	3	
3	Risk 3	4	1	
Operational:				
4	Risk 4	3	4	
5	Risk 5	3	1	
6	Risk 6	4	2	
Financial:				
7	Risk 7	1	1	
8	Risk 8	2	3	
	Etc.			

Once this has been completed we can use the risk matrix (see next page) to assign a risk rating for each risk, based on the combination of the likelihood and impact. When using a numbering system such as we are here, a common approach, as you will see from the risk matrix, is to simply multiply the two together (e.g. a risk with a likelihood of 3 and an impact of 2 results in a risk rating of 6).

The risk matrix

The risk matrix helps us to rate the significance of our identified risks based on the likelihood of the risk materialising and the impact if it does.

There are various sizes and types of risk matrix, depending on the rating scale chosen. The simplest form uses a 3 x 3 grid, but you could use a 4 x 4 or a 5 x 5 grid, or whatever you like, depending on how complicated or simple you want to make things. As described in the previous section, you can use a low, medium, high or a simple numbered scale – whichever you feel most comfortable with. A couple of examples are shown below:

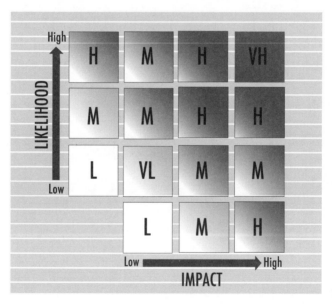

In the matrix above, at the one extreme, a low likelihood combined with a low impact results in a rating of "very low" (or, alternatively, "negligible"). At the other extreme, a high likelihood combined with a high impact results in a rating of "very high" (or, alternatively, "unacceptable").

For the purposes of the risk assessment in this book, we're using the 4 x 4 matrix shown overleaf, and rather than highs, mediums and lows, we're using a simple numbering system of 1 to 4 for the likelihood and impact axes.

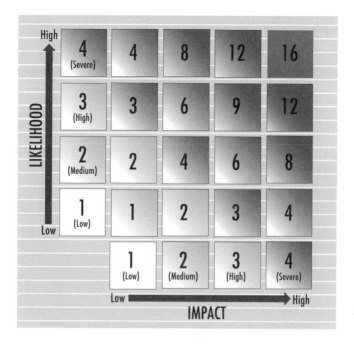

One advantage of the 4 x 4 grid over a 3 x 3 version is that it stops people being non-committal and plumping for the middle ground, while still keeping things simple. Also, some people like a "score" rather than the seemingly more subjective words as it looks a little more scientific, insofar as we multiply the likelihood and impact numbers together to arrive at the risk rating. But, actually, it doesn't really matter. Because when we look at likelihood and impact, we're really trying to determine which are the most significant of the risks – in other words, which are the ones that are most likely to happen, and which are the ones with the most serious consequences. The important thing here is that the risks we're most interested in, and that we really ought to do something about, are those that fall in the top right-hand corner and the ones that we're least bothered about fall in the bottom left.

It can be helpful to colour code the squares in the matrix green, amber and red, to indicate the seriousness and priority for action for any given risk, and to carry this colour coding through to our risk register (see page 78).

The next step is to add the risk rating (which, as we now know is a combination of the likelihood and impact) to the final column for each of our risks. This is simply a case of multiplying the likelihood and impact values, or alternatively referring to the risk matrix we saw earlier.

It's common practice – in fact it's common sense – that a "rule" is adopted whereby any risk over a certain rating (in this case we'll say 8 or more), or falling in a red square if we've colour coded them, **must** be dealt with in some way.

#	Risk	Likelihood	Impact	Rating
Commercial:				
1	Risk 1	1	2	2
2	Risk 2	3	3	9
3	Risk 3	4	1	4
Operational:				
4	Risk 4	3	4	12
5	Risk 5	3	1	3
6	Risk 6	4	2	8
Financial:				
7	Risk 7	1	1	1
8	Risk 8	2	3	6
	Etc.			

"Always look for the calculations that go with the calculated risks."

Unknown (maxim for politicians from the US Congressional Record)

Work sheet

If you completed the work sheet in chapter 2, on page 35 (and if you didn't, why not go back and do so now?), take a few moments to consider the likelihood and impact and the resulting rating for the risks that you identified, and for any others that you've subsequently thought of.

Ref	Risk	Likelihood	Impact	Rating

Later on in the book we'll look in more detail at some of the countermeasures that we might consider implementing to mitigate the risks that we consider to be significant.

Significant risks

The risk rating (a combination of the likelihood and impact) is effectively a rating of the significance of each identified risk. As discussed previously, it's the most significant risks – those towards the top right-hand corner of our risk matrix (see page 49) – that we should be most interested in and that we now need to focus our attention on mitigating.

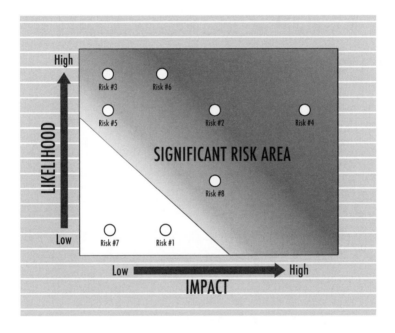

In reality, the boundary separating what we consider to be significant and insignificant risks is more likely to be a wobbly line than a straight one and its position will largely depend on the organisation's risk appetite[6] (see also "**Setting the corporate risk appetite**" on page 88).

---

[6] BS31100, the *Risk Management Code of Practice* from the British Standards Institution defines risk appetite as the "amount and type of risk that an organization is prepared to seek, accept or tolerate".

The possible measures that we can take to mitigate our significant risks are many and varied, and will depend on such factors as the type of risk, its rating and the level of investment that we're willing to make versus the potential downside. The identification and implementation of risk mitigation measures, also known as countermeasures, are discussed in more detail in the next two chapters.

Hints and tips

Analysis paralysis...

The risk assessment is a key step in the risk management process. It provides the basis for identifying, justifying, selecting and implementing our specific mitigation measures.

But it is possible to get too hung up on the analysis, with the result that subsequent activities are seriously delayed. It's usually because those doing the analysis try to be too precise or too scientific. They get bogged down in detail and lose sight of the fact that the analysis is the means to an end, not the end itself.

But where risk management is concerned, it's often better to be roughly right than precisely wrong.

So keep it simple, avoid the proverbial "analysis paralysis", and aim to get things roughly right.

Follow-up actions

This page is for you to note any key points or thoughts prompted by the content of the previous chapter and the follow-up actions you intend to take to help you manage risks in your business.

Section/page	Key points	Follow-up actions

Chapter 4 looks at the third stage in the risk management process – identifying countermeasures.

In this chapter we consider:

- The types of risk response options that apply to the various categories of risk;
- Stage 3 of the risk management process – identifying countermeasures;
- Some of the countermeasures that you might employ to mitigate your particular risks.

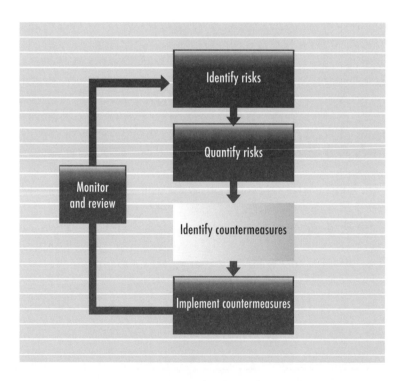

Addressing our risks

Once we've assessed the various risks to our business, we can decide what we want to do about them, prioritising our actions based on the risk rating. Clearly we'll want to concentrate first on those significant risks that fall in the top right hand corner of our risk matrix. We may also choose to address some of the less significant risks, particularly if it's easy or inexpensive to do so. As we move towards the bottom left hand corner there may well be risks that we choose to accept. Another way of looking at it is illustrated below:

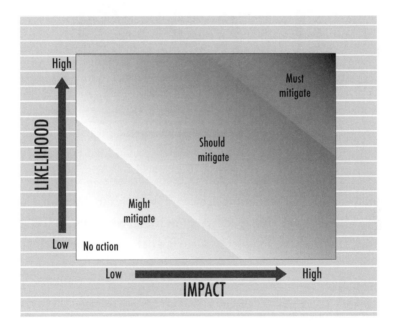

So that we can decide what actions to take, we first need to consider some of the possible mitigation measures, otherwise known as countermeasures.

Risk response options

In general terms, the responses to our various risks can largely be divided into four categories, depending on the likelihood of the risk materialising and the impact if it does. It should be noted, however, that there may be some overlap or blurring of the edges because, as with so many things in life, it's not always possible to divide things up into neat little boxes. For instance, transferring risks or insuring against them might apply to risks in either of the two right-most quadrants in the diagram below:

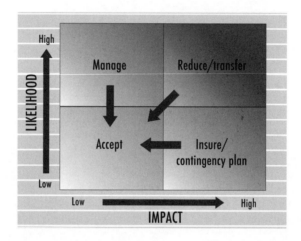

Whichever category a particular risk falls into, the ultimate aim is to select and implement measures that reduce the likelihood or impact (or both) to a level that we are prepared to accept. The four categories, along with some of the specific risk response options for each, are described in more detail on the following pages.

Risk acceptance

If the likelihood is low and the impact is low, it may be a perfectly reasonable decision to do nothing and to accept certain risks. There may also be occasions when, although there is a higher likelihood or impact, it is either uneconomic or even impossible to implement countermeasures, for instance where the cost of addressing the risk outweighs the potential loss.

In this event, the only viable option may be to accept the risk. As long as this is an informed decision, it is a perfectly valid one. The fact that many risks can't be completely eliminated means that there is likely to be a level of residual risk remaining, even after implementing our mitigation measures (see page 76). The ultimate aim of an effective risk management programme is to reduce all of our risks to a level that we are willing to accept.

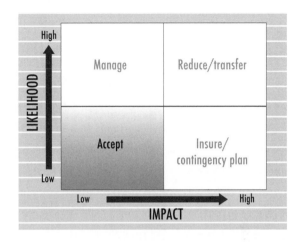

Management

For risks with a higher likelihood but a low impact (such as pilfering of low value items, minor operator errors or other "glitches" which cause inconvenience as opposed to significant problems), a sensible approach might be to manage and control them, for instance by improving and documenting processes, by providing adequate training and education and by implementing controls and procedures to regularly monitor and review the situation.

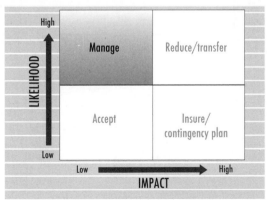

> *"It is impossible to make anything foolproof because fools are so ingenious."*

Unknown

Contingency planning

If the likelihood is low but the impact is high – such as loss of operational capability, serious damage to our reputation, large financial losses or even failure of the business – contingency plans should be developed. Often referred to as business continuity (or in some cases disaster recovery) plans, the purpose of contingency plans is to ensure that our business-critical functions or processes can continue to an acceptable, perhaps emergency, level in the (hopefully unlikely) event of some sort of catastrophic disruption. While we all hope that this type of event will never occur, spending a little time and effort considering what's important to the business and thinking through alternative means of providing them will pay dividends if the worst does happen.

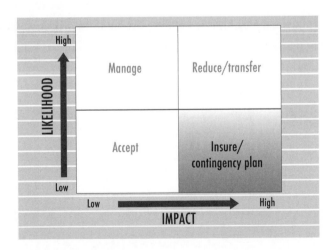

Some obvious examples of the types of risk mitigated by contingency planning include fire, flood or explosion, but it may also be prudent to consider risks such as the loss of a major customer, changes to the business environment, our marketplace, or in consumer behaviour, product contamination, bad publicity, failure of critical equipment, loss of key staff and a range of other potential "disasters".

Contingency plans may include such things as:
- Evacuation;
- Crisis or incident management;
- Communication with customers and other stakeholders (including the media);
- Sourcing alternative premises, plant or equipment;
- Relocation and recovery of critical business functions and their supporting infrastructure or services;
- Alternative means of supply and/or distribution.

...and a number of other things which will vary from business to business.

However, while contingency plans are a very good idea, it's always worth remembering that the old adage "prevention is better than cure" holds good if prevention is at all possible – after all, it's far better not to have a disaster in the first place if it can be avoided!

> *"We are ready for any unforeseen event that may or may not occur."*
>
> **George W. Bush, former US President**

Case study

A retail business with a warehouse in Hemel Hempstead had given some thought as to how they would continue operations in the event of a catastrophic failure, such as a fire, flood or denial of access. Their contingency planning included identifying the key people who would manage the response and recovery activities following such an incident, training them and carrying out an exercise to check that the plan would work.

Incredibly, just three days after the exercise, they were glad they'd done their homework as they had to do it all again for real when a series of explosions and a huge fire engulfed the Buncefield oil terminal, approximately half a mile away. The explosions caused severe damage to their building and the emergency services exclusion zone meant that they couldn't access it for several weeks.

Their plans worked and, unlike some of their neighbours, they were able to relocate and continue their critical operations in a rented warehouse elsewhere within days of the incident.

Risk reduction

For risks with a high likelihood and a high impact, risk reduction measures are absolutely essential. For instance, hazardous or dangerous procedures should be modified, stringently controlled and monitored or outsourced to someone more qualified or better equipped to carry them out safely (see **"Transferring risk"** overleaf). In extreme cases, if the potential downsides far outweigh the potential benefits, a decision to discontinue the activity altogether may be considered.

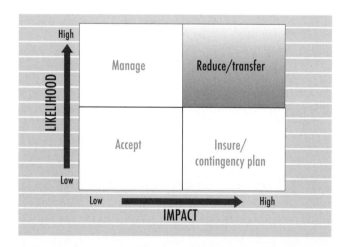

More information on specific countermeasures within the various categories can be found in the next section.

Identifying countermeasures

For risks that we're unwilling or unable to accept, there are numerous possible countermeasures, or mitigation measures, that we may consider, within the categories of reduction, management and contingency planning described in the previous section.

The specific countermeasures we select to address each risk will vary depending upon the type of risk, its rating, our risk appetite (see page 88) and our budget, but may involve steps to transfer, reduce or control the risk. Some of the possible countermeasures are shown below.

Transferring risk

Transferring the risk to someone else can be achieved by taking out insurance or perhaps by outsourcing certain high risk or "non-core" activities or processes. Remember though, that outsourcing carries its own risks, which also need to be assessed before making a decision. You need to be fully aware of what's being provided by the outsourcing arrangement (and what's not) and where the risks lie, as you may still need to put in place some mitigation measures. You might also want to satisfy yourself that the outsourcer takes their risk management seriously and that they have a contingency (business continuity) plan in place.

And remember too, that as far as your customers and other stakeholders are concerned the buck stops with you, not the outsourced supplier.

Hints and tips

A source of embarrassment...

Many businesses choose to outsource certain activities, for various reasons. They may consider them to be non-core activities, want to outsource a particularly specialist or risky process, or do it purely to save money.

Outsourcing can make good commercial sense, but only if the implications and risks are properly understood.

Several businesses have suffered serious embarrassment or damage to their reputation owing to an outsourcer's failure to deliver. Whether it's IT, manufacturing, delivery, call centres, purchasing or whatever, someone else's problem can quickly become yours.

If things go wrong your customers will turn to you, not the outsourcer. You might have outsourced the process, but you retain the risk ... and the responsibility ... and the reputation ... and the hassle if things go wrong.

So make sure your decision to outsource is an informed one. One that includes a thorough risk and impact assessment and an understanding of the outsourcer's own risk management capability and contingency plans.

Insurance

Insurance is a common, and extremely important, form of risk management. Depending on the specifics of your particular business and your personal circumstances, certain types of insurance will be necessary or desirable. There are many types of insurance, some of which are listed below. Insurance is, however, a complex area and professional advice should be sought as to the specific types and levels of insurance that you should consider for your business.

- Buildings and contents;
- Goods in transit;
- Business interruption;
- Consequential loss;
- Directors' and officers (D&O) insurance;
- Increased cost of working;
- Employers', public and product liability;
- Professional indemnity;
- Loss of profits;
- Warranty insurance;
- Legal expenses;
- Life and health;
- Motor vehicles;
- Engineering insurance (electrical or mechanical breakdown);
- Money (cash, cheques, etc. on the premises, at employees homes and in transit);
- Credit risk;
- "Key person" insurance;
- Income protection;
- Travel insurance;

- Personal accident and sickness;
- Private medical insurance.

Case study

Computer disks, which had previously belonged to a hospital trust, bought second-hand at an online auction site were found to contain sensitive and confidential data, including patients' medical records and personnel details.

The disks had been disposed of by the trust via their contract with an external company, who should have erased the data. In fact, only a basic level of deletion had been carried out and the data was still accessible using standard data analysis tools.

While the problem resulted from the supplier not carrying out their contractual obligations properly, it was the hospital trust that received the negative media attention and risked legal action from their patients and staff.

The trust subsequently carried out a review of its policies and has stated that it no longer uses external companies to dispose of IT equipment.

(Source: BBC news – www.bbc.co.uk/news)

Footnote: it is estimated that between 40% and 50% of second-hand disks contain sensitive data that has not been effectively deleted.

Insurance may provide a safety net for your business if things go horribly wrong, but do bear in mind that insurance only addresses (some of) the financial impacts of some of your risks. It merely provides a pre-defined sum of money in the event that certain pre-defined risks occur. It almost certainly won't pay out immediately – in fact, experience has shown that insurance can take months, or even years, to pay out and that the claims process is often fraught with difficulties (strangely enough, paying out on claims isn't the favourite activity for most insurance companies!).

In the meantime, what it won't do is keep your business operating or protect your cash flow in the short term. It won't stop your customers going elsewhere or protect your market share. It won't protect your reputation or replace the goodwill you've painstakingly built up, possibly over a period of many years.

And it's a sobering thought that the sums paid out are often less than anticipated, and often don't actually cover the full value of the losses incurred. So it's vital that you clearly understand what your various insurance policies cover and, as importantly, what they don't, so that you can supplement your risk management strategy with other appropriate mitigation measures. In any case, insurance shouldn't be seen as a substitute for other mitigation measures. Often insurers will, quite reasonably, require you to have other measures in place to reduce the likelihood and/or impact of the insured risk(s) occurring – in other words, to reduce your, and their, risk of a claim arising.

The appropriate use of insurance is an important weapon in your risk management armoury, but it's a big mistake to view it as the only weapon. And it should be seen as the last line of defence, rather than the first.

Risk reduction and control

Risk reduction and control measures may include (though are not limited to) the following[7]:

Strategic:
- Multiple locations (e.g. production, warehousing, offices);
- Market intelligence/research;
- Joint ventures/partnerships;
- Divestment (e.g. unprofitable/non-core business);
- Diversification;
- Cessation of high risk activities.

Operational:
- Fire detection and suppression;
- Physical security measures (e.g. security guards, intruder detection, access control, etc.);
- Duplication of, or built-in redundancy in critical equipment or functions;
- Regular maintenance;
- Policies and procedures – ensuring things are done in a certain way, every time;
- Buffer stocks;
- Automation;
- Stock control and regular stock checks;
- Alternative/multiple suppliers;
- Quality assurance;
- Documentation.

[7] The risk reduction and control measures are shown under the various categories (strategic, operational, financial, etc.) for illustrative purposes. Some measures may, in reality, apply to more than one category or may fall under a different category in your particular environment.

Financial/commercial:

- Customer relationship management;
- Authorisation levels/purchasing limits;
- Contractual terms and conditions;
- Financial controls;
- Cash flow management;
- Credit limits and credit references;
- Overdraft facilities;
- Hedging;
- Cost control;
- Futures/options;
- Factoring/invoice discounting;
- Segregation of duties/processes (e.g. authorisation from payment).

Regulatory/compliance:

- Due diligence;
- Monitoring and reporting.

Health and safety:

- Evacuation procedures;
- Personal protective equipment;
- Safety devices/guards on equipment/machinery;
- Health and safety reviews and targeted risk assessments;
- Safe systems of working;
- Good housekeeping.

Personnel:

- Employing suitably skilled/experienced staff and contractors;
- Background checks on new employees;
- Supervision;
- Training (including cross-training);
- Good working conditions;
- Management reviews;
- Job rotation and succession planning;
- Good employee relations.

Technology:

- Information security measures (e.g. secure passwords, restricted access, virus checking, firewalls, etc.);
- IT backups;
- Uninterruptible power supplies or standby generators.

Project:

- Project management methodology;
- Experienced/skilled project manager(s).

The above list is by no means an exhaustive one and you may well come up with additional countermeasures that address your own particular risks.

> *"Chance favours the prepared mind."*
>
> **Louis Pasteur, French chemist and biologist**

Work sheet

If you've completed the work sheets in the previous sections, take a few moments now to list the countermeasures that you might consider to mitigate the significant risks that you've identified.

Ref	Risk	Possible countermeasure(s)	(Y/N)
		in place?	

Later on in the book we'll look at some of the issues associated with the implementation and monitoring of our selected countermeasures.

Follow-up actions

This page is for you to note any key points or thoughts prompted by the content of the previous chapter and the follow-up actions you intend to take to help you manage risks in your business.

Section/page	Key points	Follow-up actions

Chapter 5 looks at the fourth stage in the risk management process – implementing countermeasures.

In this chapter we consider:

- Stage 4 of the risk management process – implementing countermeasures;
- Residual risk – the level of risk remaining after implementing our selected countermeasures;
- Risk registers.

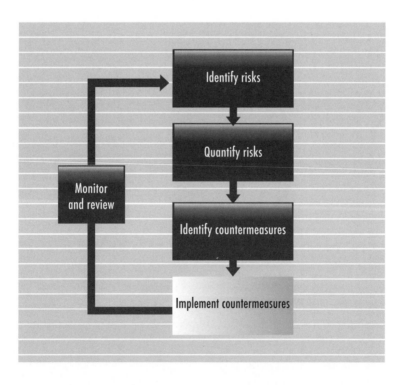

Implementing countermeasures

There's not much point in spending time and effort identifying and quantifying our risks and thinking about the countermeasures that we can implement to address them if we then do nothing else. We can assess risks until the cows come home, but it's what we then *do* about them that really matters, otherwise it's all been a bit of a waste of time. In order to make our business more resilient we now have to make some decisions and take some action. It may seem blindingly obvious, but it's an often overlooked fact that merely writing down our risks in a risk register (see page 78) won't actually protect our business or make it any more robust. So we now have to turn our attention to implementing some of those countermeasures and deciding how much time, effort and money we want to invest in mitigating our more significant risks.

No business, no matter what its size, has limitless resources to invest in risk management. In any case, there's little benefit and little sense in spending a fortune addressing a risk which is unlikely to happen and which would have minimal or no impact even if it did. On the other hand, if a risk is likely to occur that has the potential to cause significant harm or put you out of business then a substantial investment (in money, time or other resources) may be needed to reduce the likelihood and/or the impact to an acceptable level, or serious consideration should be given to whether it's a risk that's worth taking at all. The countermeasures that we choose must therefore be appropriate, pragmatic and cost-effective.

Once we've selected the countermeasures to be implemented, it's important that the implementation process is properly managed. It may be that some countermeasures are fairly quick and easy to implement, whereas others may require significant effort, cost or time. The latter type will probably need to be managed as a formal project, with all that that entails. Either way, it's important to allocate responsibility for implementing specific countermeasures, whether to a particular director or manager, a project manager or a member of staff. Often, risks are not properly mitigated because it was wrongly assumed that the proverbial "someone else" had dealt with it.

Case study

A manufacturing company had to relocate staff from one of its buildings after a car skidded off the road and crashed into the side of it, causing structural damage.

Ironically, the risk had been identified previously, but the installation of bollards as a countermeasure had not been carried out due to the cost.

Fortunately, a high-tech production line making critical components, previously housed in the building, had been relocated a few weeks previously for other operational reasons, otherwise the impact would have been far greater.

Residual risk

It's impossible to totally eliminate risk and there will almost always be some level of risk remaining after we've implemented our countermeasures. This is often referred to as residual, or net, risk (gross risk being that which exists before mitigation). As discussed previously, the aim is to end up with a level of residual risk that we're willing to accept.

It's also possible that reducing risk in one area might actually have the effect of increasing the level of risk elsewhere. Examples might include:

- A business employs a factoring company to aid cash flow, but customers are upset by the factoring company's methods of chasing payments, resulting in customer dissatisfaction and a negative impact on reputation.

- Consolidation of premises and facilities to reduce costs and improve efficiency reduces resilience and results in a single point of failure.

- Moving the production of products or components overseas to increase competitiveness results in a reduction in quality and an increase in failure rates.

- Training staff to enhance skills, increase productivity and reduce operational errors makes them more marketable and increases the risk of losing staff to competitors.

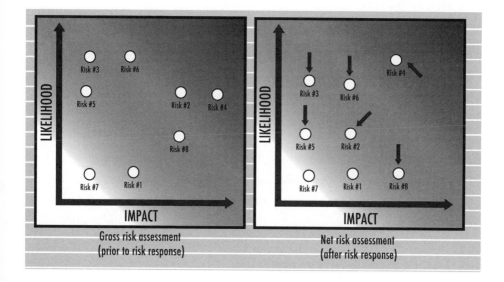

Gross risk assessment
(prior to risk response)

Net risk assessment
(after risk response)

So, while it's important to give individual risks the focus they deserve, we also need to ensure that we keep an eye on the bigger picture to ensure that our overall risk levels are acceptable (see also Chapter 6, which discusses the need for ongoing monitoring and review).

This brings into play the concept of enterprise risk management. Whether yours is a huge multinational corporation, a 5-person business or somewhere in between, a co-ordinated approach to risk management is desirable, if not essential, if the entire portfolio of risks is to be effectively managed.

 Case study

A small electrical fire in a vending machine at a printing company set off the sprinklers (installed some months previously at the behest of their insurers to reduce the risk of fire).

The vending machine fire was quickly extinguished but water from the sprinklers damaged high-tech printing equipment resulting in costs of over £250,000 and loss of printing capability for several weeks.

The risk register

The risk register is a very simple but very useful tool, which will help you to manage your risks. It's a document which summarises the risks identified, along with the likelihood, impact and the resulting risk rating and the appropriate countermeasures for each, plus the actions that you've decided to take and the current status of them.

Once you've been through the process of identifying risks, assessing their likelihood and impact and identifying countermeasures, you will have much of the information you need to create your risk register(s). All that's required is to create a table or spreadsheet similar to the example below, populate it with the information gathered from your workshop(s), then assign specific actions, with associated responsibilities and timescales.

#	Risk	Likelihood	Impact	Rating	Countermeasures	In place?	Actions/status/comments	Person responsible	Due date/complete
1	Risk 1	1	2	2	c/measure 1	Y			
2	Risk 2	3	3	9	c/measure 2	N			
3	Risk 3	4	1	4	c/measure 3 + 4	Y			
4	Risk 4	3	4	12	c/measure 5 + 6	N			
	Etc.				Etc.				

The key point here is that the risk register should be a working document that's reviewed and updated regularly, not something that's produced once and then filed away, never to be seen again.

Ideally (and depending on the size and structure of the business), each department or business function should create and maintain its own risk register, for the risks that apply to them and that they are able to do something about, with a central risk register for the business-wide or "bigger picture" risks. However, it's very much "horses for courses" and, at the end of the day, a single risk register is much better than none at all. Whether you plump for one or several, it's important that each risk register is owned by someone, who is given responsibility for its upkeep.

 Hints and tips

Accentuate the positive...

When carrying out risk assessments and creating the associated risk registers, most people tend to focus on the negatives. But not all risks are negative – some can be positive. In fact, if it wasn't for the positive risks, and the ability to successfully exploit them, there wouldn't be successful businesses.

So it follows that risk management isn't just about avoiding the bad stuff – it's also about positive risk taking. It's about balancing the potential downsides against the potential opportunities. Therefore when carrying out our risk assessments, while it's extremely important to think about those downsides, we should consider the opportunities as well as the threats.

So why not add an "opportunities" column to your risk assessment flip chart and to your risk registers and think about the potential positives as well as the negatives?

Follow-up actions

This page is for you to note any key points or thoughts prompted by the content of the previous chapter and the follow-up actions you intend to take to help you manage risks in your business.

Section/page	Key points	Follow-up actions

Chapter 6 looks at the final stage of the risk management process – ongoing monitoring and reviewing.

In this chapter we consider:

- Stage 5 of the risk management process – ongoing monitoring and reviewing;

- Assessing the effectiveness of our selected countermeasures;

- The appointment of a risk group to monitor risks and associated actions across the business as a whole;

- The organisation's risk appetite;

- The benefits of a risk-aware culture and the roles of key groups of people in embedding one.

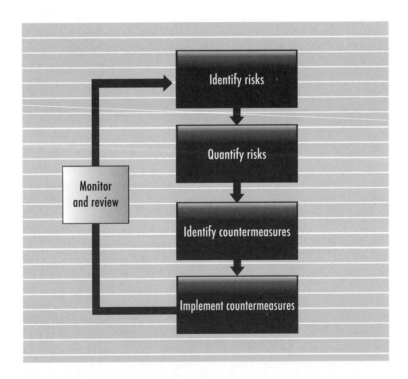

Monitoring and reviewing

The final stage in the risk management process is to monitor and evaluate the results of our risk mitigation measures.

For each countermeasure put in place we should consider whether:

• It does the job it's intended to do.	To what extent does it address the risk? If it doesn't do the job fully, can we do anything to improve things?
• It reduces our overall exposure to risk.	In some cases, too much focus on reducing one risk can actually increase other risks. We need to be aware of this, avoid being too blinkered and consider the bigger picture too.
• It improves efficiency.	In addition to mitigating specific risks, modifying and improving processes, procedures and working practices can often have a positive effect on the day to day running of the business by reducing operational errors, failures or outages and increasing efficiency.
• It continues to be cost effective.	Do we reach a point where the cost outweighs the benefit? If so, is there anything we can do to improve the situation? Or should we drop it and consider other mitigation measures instead?

- The level of residual risk is acceptable. This is not a decision to be taken lightly. Bear in mind that accepting a risk also means acceptance of the consequences if it does occur.

- It's being adhered to. If the countermeasure requires a process or procedure to be followed, or some other form of manual intervention, is it being carried out correctly and consistently? Merely assuming that it is could be risky – you need to regularly check and monitor the situation.

"It is clear that risk management is now a core business process and should be planned accordingly and on a continuing basis so as to reduce risk and volatility and improve returns."

Institute of Chartered Accountants in England and Wales

There's an old adage that "what gets measured gets done", so it's important that we review and assess the effectiveness of our risk mitigation measures. There are a number of ways in which this can be done. For instance, we might look at the following metrics:

- Financial measurements, e.g.:
  - Cash flow
  - Revenue
  - Costs
  - Profit margins

- Operational measurements, e.g.:
  - Service delivery
  - Productivity
  - Quality control
  - Equipment/IT failure
  - Operator errors
  - Accidents
  - Downtime

- Commercial measurements, e.g.:
  - Increased sales
  - Lost sales
  - Contractual issues

- Customer feedback, e.g.:
  - Customer service ratings
  - Complaints
  - Accolades
  - Repeat business

As well as keeping an eye on the effectiveness of our risk control measures and identifying changes or improvements to existing countermeasures, regular monitoring and review will ensure that new and emerging risks, changes to existing risks and new opportunities are captured and addressed appropriately.

The frequency will vary depending on a number of factors, including the type of business you're in, the rate of change (both within the business and within the environment or marketplace in which it operates), the type of risks and the specific controls implemented and any regulatory requirements (for instance, health and safety legislation requires certain risks to be periodically reviewed or re-assessed when certain changes occur).

The main point is that this should be an iterative process, rather than a one-off exercise if risks are to be effectively managed.

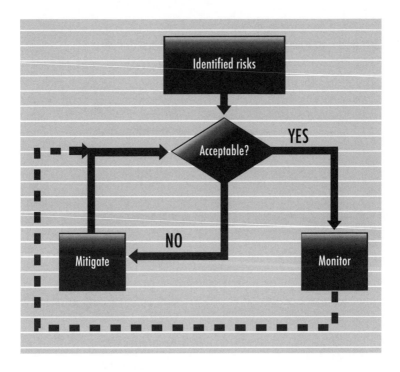

Most reviews are carried out internally, and regular internal reviews or audits have a key part to play in the risk assessment process. It may, however, also be beneficial to obtain an independent assessment from external experts from time to time. Indeed, in some cases external audit of the effectiveness of controls may be a regulatory or statutory requirement.

Joining it all up

In order to ensure that risks are managed in a consistent way across the business, rather than in isolated pockets, it can be beneficial to appoint some form of risk management steering group. Indeed, many organisations employ this approach very successfully as part of their risk management structure.

The size and composition of the group and the frequency with which it meets are likely to vary from business to business, but it usually comprises management representatives from each key area[8] and reports directly to the Board or senior management team. This reporting usually includes identification of the key risks (often the top ten) facing the business and updates on the status of these risks.

The role of the risk management steering group is to monitor risks and associated actions across the business as a whole, ensuring that key risks affecting more than one area or those that can't be addressed by a single department or function are escalated and treated appropriately. The advantages include:

- A consistent, co-ordinated, business-wide approach to risk management;

- Consideration of "the bigger picture" and monitoring of the overall level of risk;

- A strategic, as well as tactical, view of risk;

- Key risks being given the focus and attention that they deserve, including awareness at the highest level of management.

[8] In a larger business this might include representatives from Operations, Finance, Commercial, Customer Services, HR, and/or various other functions, whereas in a smaller business one person may represent more than one business area.

Setting the corporate risk appetite

People are individuals and we all have our own particular appetite for risk. Some people are extreme risk takers who think nothing of taking huge risks, both in their business and personal lives, which the mere mortals among us would cringe at the very thought of. Others are far more reserved, to the point of being almost totally risk averse, avoiding almost any situation in which there is even the slightest hint of risk. The vast majority of us fall somewhere in between.

Similarly, all organisations have a "corporate" risk appetite, which dictates the types and levels of risk that the organisation, or at least the Board or senior management team that directs it, are willing to take or to accept. Indeed, one of the key roles of the Board or senior management team is to decide on the level of downside risk that the business is willing to take in seeking to exploit opportunities. The problem is that it can be very difficult to pin them down and get them to define the corporate risk appetite, partly because it's quite difficult to put into words and partly because it's actually quite subjective and can change depending on factors such as the prevailing business environment, the timing, or even the personalities, personal experiences or professional (or emotional) judgement of the decision makers. So few organisations bother to do so, and fewer still actually document and publish a formal statement of risk appetite to their managers and staff, which can make life a bit difficult for them in terms of their own risk management efforts.

While it's not always possible to come up with a clearly defined and agreed statement of the corporate risk appetite before embarking on your risk management programme, it's a good idea for the Board or senior management team to give some direction on the levels of risk that they're willing to accept and those which they aren't – for instance the level of financial, customer service, reputation, and other types of impact that they're comfortable with.

One way of doing this is to agree with them what the risk matrix should look like; to at least help define the boundaries for the green, amber and red segments. Once the significant risks (particularly the "bigger picture" ones) have been identified and quantified, they should be asked for confirmation (ideally in writing as this always helps to focus the mind!) of which specific risks they are willing to accept and which they want to address in some way.

It's entirely possible that the acceptable levels of risk will vary from one risk category to another – for instance, a high level of strategic or equipment risk or opportunity risk may be acceptable, whereas the opposite may well be true of health and safety or reputational risk. In this case, an effective way of approaching it is to ask for clarification of the acceptable levels of risk in each of the various categories, as illustrated in the diagram below:

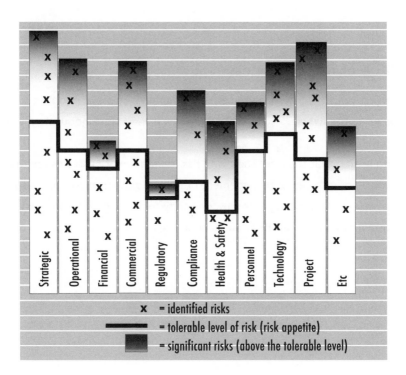

x = identified risks
━━━ = tolerable level of risk (risk appetite)
▇ = significant risks (above the tolerable level)

Whichever approach is taken, getting a steer from those at the top can be hugely beneficial. It helps to get their buy-in, ensures a consistent approach, makes the risk assessment process more productive and can potentially save a significant amount of wasted time and effort by preventing managers and staff from barking up the proverbial wrong tree.

> *"The early bird catches the worm, but the second mouse gets the cheese."*
>
> Unknown

A culture of risk awareness

A key objective of the risk management programme is to make people risk aware, as opposed to risk averse, and to embed that awareness throughout the business.

It's worth noting that the most successful risk management processes are those that involve not only senior management but all employees. Involving people, raising awareness and giving them responsibility for managing the risks within their control can have a significant impact on the overall resilience of the business.

To this end, various people within the business have various roles to play. Depending on the size and nature of the business these key groups, and their associated roles and responsibilities, may include:

Directors/senior management:

- Visibly support the risk management process;

- Agree and publish a risk management policy, setting out the scope, objectives, roles and responsibilities;

- Set and communicate the organisation's risk appetite (acceptable levels of risk);

- Be aware of significant risks, in particular strategic risks, facing the business;

- Monitor the effectiveness of the risk management process;

- Report to stakeholders on the effectiveness of the risk management process in achieving the business's strategic objectives.

Risk management steering group:

- Support and facilitate the risk management process;

- Monitor risks and associated activities across the business;

- Report on the status of key risks and mitigation measures to the Board/executive management team;

- Ensure appropriate levels of awareness and involvement throughout the business.

Business managers/team leaders:

- Be aware of the risks within their particular area of responsibility;

- Apply the risk management process to identify significant risks and implement or recommend mitigation measures;

- Manage risks on a day-to-day basis;

- Facilitate staff awareness;

- Report on the status of risks and mitigation measures to the directors/senior management (perhaps via the risk management steering group).

Individuals:

- Understand their roles, responsibilities and accountabilities within the risk management process;

- Identify and rate risks and suggest possible mitigation measures;

- Report on the status of risks and mitigation measures to team leaders/business managers.

Joining forces...

Risk management is much more effective if a top down and bottom up approach is adopted. It's all very well for executive management to make statements in the annual report about how wonderful the risk management system is, but that in itself doesn't make the organisation more resilient. If it isn't backed up by action then it's not worth the paper it's written on.

A successful risk management approach requires a two-pronged attack, which includes buy-in from both the executive and business managers. Yes, there needs to be commitment at Board level, but the operational parts of the business also need to be involved to make it happen.

The most successful organisations in this respect are the ones who manage to embed risk management in their culture – where executive support is visible; where risks and associated mitigation measures are identified at all levels; where risk registers are maintained by departmental managers and team leaders; and where risk management is seen by all employees as just a normal part of the way they do their jobs.

So what's it to be – splendid isolation or a joined-up approach that actually makes a difference? The choice is yours.

The wider context

It's potentially useful to note that, in addition to your own business's risk assessment efforts, risks are also being assessed in a wider context by a number of organisations as part of the UK's national risk register process, driven by the Civil Contingencies Act[9].

Each area of the UK (based on police force boundaries) has a "Local Resilience Forum" comprising representatives from the various "emergency responders" and supporting agencies defined by the Civil Contingencies Act (emergency services, local authorities, health bodies and government agencies), the purpose of which is to facilitate consultation, collaboration and disclosure of information with each other in order to facilitate planning and response to emergencies.

Each Local Resilience Forum is required to undertake risk assessments, for risks that could result in a major emergency, and to maintain a community risk register for the area that it represents. This community risk register is seen as the first step in the emergency planning process, as it ensures that the plans that are developed are proportionate to the risk. The Civil Contingencies Act includes a statutory obligation for these community risk registers to be made public, usually via each Local Resilience Forum website, which means that businesses are able to gain an awareness of the wider risk agenda.

[9] The Civil Contingencies Act is a UK Act of Parliament that came into force in 2005 to replace the previous Civil Defence and Emergency Powers legislation. The stated aim of the Civil Contingencies Act is to "deliver a single framework for civil protection in the UK capable of meeting the challenges of the 21st century". Part 1 of the Act focuses on local arrangements for civil protection, establishing a statutory framework of roles and responsibilities for "local responders". Part 2 focuses on emergency powers to deal with the effects of the most serious emergencies.

This page is for you to note any key points or thoughts prompted by the content of the previous chapter and the follow-up actions you intend to take to help you manage risks in your business.

Section/page	Key points	Follow-up actions

Chapter 7 looks at a few useful tools and techniques that can aid the risk management process.

Some tools and techniques worth considering

There are a number of tools and techniques available that can help us to manage our risks. There are others that some may say over-complicate the process and largely fall into the category of "useful" for the professional risk manager, who has the luxury of being able to devote his or her full time and attention to the subject.

Because the purpose of this book is to simplify and demystify the risk management process and make it more relevant to those who feel it's important but for whom it isn't necessarily a full-time occupation, there's no room for most of them here! However, there are a few techniques that are worthy of consideration and therefore worth a few words here.

Brainstorming

Brainstorming is an extremely popular technique which involves thinking quickly and creatively. This is achieved via an intensive, facilitated group discussion, the theory being that by not allowing time for reflection, creative ideas can be generated and problem-solving stimulated. Brainstorming is a very effective technique for the early stages of the risk management process, specifically for the identification of risks and possible countermeasures.

A tried and trusted method of brainstorming risks is to write down the risk categories (e.g. strategic, commercial, financial, operational, technical, etc., as discussed on pages 29 and 30) as headings and, taking the categories one at a time, ask each person in turn to identify a risk. Write it on the flipchart then move onto the next. If someone doesn't have a contribution during a particular round, don't make a fuss, just move on to the next person, then the next until someone does identify a risk. When no-one has anything to add, move on to the next category and continue in this fashion until all the categories have been exhausted and/or everyone's had enough.

Smaller businesses (particularly the proverbial "one man band") may feel that brainstorming isn't for them as it is, by definition, a group activity. However, they might just have to be a bit creative here and involve people from outside the business. Brainstorming risks doesn't necessarily require an in-depth knowledge of the business by everyone involved – all that's really required is a bit of imagination and a willingness to participate. So besides employees, enlisting the help of friends or family members, ex-colleagues, business associates, trusted customers or suppliers might all be viable options.

Dependency modelling

Dependency modelling is an extremely useful technique. As the name suggests, it's a way of mapping dependencies, showing where failure in one area can impact upon others. Its strengths are in its simplicity and its versatility. It can be used to highlight the dependencies in a whole host of situations, for instance within systems, processes or environments, between pieces of equipment, facilities or other assets. It can be used to show the dependencies associated with meeting a particular objective or even to map the dependencies across the business as a whole. A simple example of a dependency model is shown below.

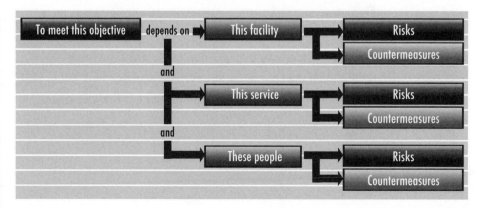

One advantage of a dependency model is that it defines what is to be achieved, what needs to be in place or done in order to achieve it and what those things depend upon. Doing this helps us to prioritise and to focus on particular areas of concern. Dependency modelling helps us to:

- Put the identified risks into an operational context;

- Capture all the risks in a particular activity, system, process or project;

- Show which risks have the potential to cause the most problems;

- Justify the recommended countermeasures or courses of action;

- Show which countermeasures are likely to be the most effective;

- Encourage further investigation of sensitive areas.

There are software packages available that provide additional "bells and whistles", including detailed probability and impact data and complex calculations, but in its simplest form a dependency model can be drawn on a piece of paper (or using an off the shelf drawing package on your PC).

Dependency modelling can be used in conjunction with the risk management process, either before, after, or even as part of the risk assessment workshop. Mapping the dependencies within a particular system or process before conducting the risk assessment can help to focus the minds of participants on the key areas of risk. Alternatively, creating a dependency model for the key risks identified by the risk assessment can help ensure that you don't overlook something important when determining the countermeasures to be implemented. Either way, dependency modelling can be a great help in ensuring that our risk assessment efforts are targeted effectively.

Process mapping

Process mapping has many applications, one of which is to understand the various inputs, outputs, linkages and dependencies within a process or system.

In a risk management context this can be very useful for highlighting single points of failure or for ensuring that an important element of a process or system isn't overlooked when considering its associated risks.

Process mapping doesn't have to be hugely complex, but you do need to consider all of the key elements within the process that is being mapped. Process maps can be drawn left to right (as in figure a) or top to bottom (as in figure b), and can contain as much or as little information as you want to include. They can be created using "standard" process map or flow chart symbols (as in figure b) or simple boxes (as figure a).

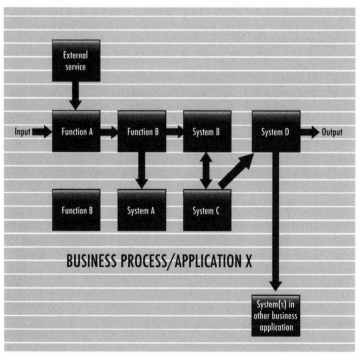

Figure a

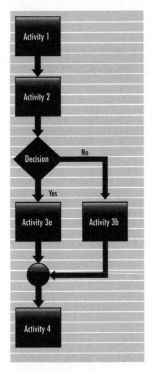

Figure b

The map on the previous page shows the various functions and systems within a particular business process and the interrelationships between them. A similar map could just as easily show the IT systems or pieces of hardware within a particular business application, the equipment and processes within a manufacturing plant or the key components that go to make up a product or service.

Used in conjunction with the risk assessment, process mapping can, like dependency modelling, (albeit in a slightly different way), help us to focus our efforts on what's important to our key processes, applications or systems.

SWOT analysis

SWOT Analysis is a method of evaluating the *strengths, weaknesses, opportunities* and *threats* associated with an activity or entity. SWOT analysis is often used in project management, but it can be used to examine practically anything – a product or service, an activity, function or process, a project, a new business venture, an investment, a competitor, a facility, an organisation, a team or even an individual.

SWOT analysis often begins by specifying the objective to be achieved and looks at the internal and external factors that can impact (either positively or negatively) on achieving that objective. It can be a useful aid to identifying areas for further development, including:

- Exploiting and capitalising on existing strengths;

- Improving on areas of weakness.

The results of the analysis are often presented in the form of a matrix or a simple table, such as:

Strengths	Weaknesses
Strength A	Weakness A
Strength B	
Opportunities	**Threats**
Opportunity A	Threat A
Opportunity B	Threat B
Opportunity C	

or

Strengths	Weaknesses	Opportunities	Threats
Strength A	Weakness A	Opportunity A	Threat A
Strength B		Opportunity B	Threat B
		Opportunity C	

From a risk management perspective, SWOT analysis can be a useful aid in:

- Identifying threats and vulnerabilities;

- Assessing the relative merits of the various countermeasures under consideration;

- Analysing the effectiveness of existing mitigation measures;

- Monitoring results and identifying corrective actions or improvements.

"The chief executive who knows his strengths and weaknesses... is likely to be far more effective than the one who remains blind to them."

John Adair, leadership trainer

Follow-up actions

This page is for you to note any key points or thoughts prompted by the content of the previous chapter and the follow-up actions you intend to take to help you manage risks in your business.

Section/page	Key points	Follow-up actions

Chapter 8 brings things to a conclusion and suggests
what your next steps might be.

Where do we go from here?

Your risk assessment will have identified a number of risks and associated mitigation measures. Some of these mitigation measures will be achievable without requiring significant resource or expenditure, while others may require considerable financial investment and may take some time to implement. The level of investment that you are prepared to make and the level of residual risk that you are prepared to live with can only be decided by you and your management team. They will depend on available funds, the strategic view of senior management and the corporate risk appetite. However, once risks have been identified they cannot simply be ignored. You must now decide, and sign up to, which risks you are willing to accept and which you are not.

It should be borne in mind that effective risk management is an ongoing process rather than merely a one-off exercise, which needs the active involvement of people across the whole business. It's therefore important that the risks identified are managed and monitored, and also that risk assessments are conducted regularly as part of the project or change management processes, when making key strategic or operational decisions and, quite simply, as a component of good management practice.

The transition to the more formalised and regular approach suggested in this book should not be overly onerous, provided that you keep things simple. It does, however, require senior management support and although this will entail some effort, the potential rewards include a more robust and resilient business that's more likely to achieve its strategic goals and objectives.

If you've picked up just one thing from this book that has prompted you to think seriously about a significant risk, or risks, to your business, then reading it has been time well spent. But that's not really enough. By definition, if a risk is significant, then something really should be done to mitigate it. Therefore, if you now take no further action you're not only missing a trick, but you're knowingly putting your business at risk.

So, if you haven't already done so, why not take a little bit of time to think about the countermeasures you can sensibly put in place, then complete the risk management process by implementing them and monitoring them for effectiveness? Your business will be that much stronger as a result and it might just help you to sleep better at night!

The rest, as they say, is up to you.

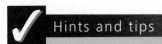

The downside of being a successful risk manager...

The trouble with managing risks successfully is that the benefits often go unnoticed. When things go horribly wrong it can be very visible, sometimes quite dramatic, sometimes quite distressing. But when we avoid things going wrong people are generally none the wiser. And people generally don't give much thought to the risk that never occurs.

Consider the example of a production manager in a manufacturing company who recognises the risk of a hazardous chemical spill. He carries out a risk assessment and concludes that, owing to current working practices, there is a high risk of a spill occurring, the consequences of which would be extremely serious. So he convinces the board that processes need to be tightened and staff need to be trained. The board finally agree, although they aren't particularly happy about the cost. Rigorous new procedures are implemented, resulting in complaints from staff who thought the old ways were fine and who are unhappy that the new processes take more time and effort. A programme of training is carried out, which team leaders complain about because it takes staff away from day to day operations for a short time. Pretty much all the production manager gets for his trouble is grief. But, as a result of his actions, the chemical spill doesn't occur, no-one dies, the factory isn't closed down by the Health and Safety Executive, the reputation of the company remains intact, the workforce still have jobs and none of the Board are prosecuted or sued.

You'd think the production manager would be hailed as a hero, but sadly in real life that just doesn't happen.

So if being a hero is your aim, forget about managing your risks – you'd be better off letting things go horribly wrong so that you can demonstrate your heroism in the face of adversity! Or you could just take the quiet satisfaction of knowing that, because of your efforts, no-one had to be a hero after all.

Conclusion

If properly done, risk management is a wise investment. It can help us when planning and starting up our new business ventures and during our ongoing business operations. It can help us to increase the chances of successfully exploiting new opportunities and the resulting risk reduction and resilience measures can pay dividends by improving processes and reducing the occurrence of everyday problems. Risk management can help us ensure that we have the correct types and levels of insurance in place. It can give us the confidence that as far as possible we are safeguarding our businesses and our livelihoods from the threat of failure, disruption or disaster.

We can't avoid risk. But we can manage it to our advantage. The most effective way to do this is to make risk management part of the business's culture. Whether it employs just a few, a few dozen or hundreds of people, your business needs to manage its risks and everyone in the business has a part to play, from the chief executive to the office junior.

By using a few simple techniques, as described in this book, each of us can identify the risks to our part of the business and the countermeasures that can be put in place to reduce the likelihood and/or the impact of the most serious, thus strengthening each part of the business.

Risk management isn't just the domain of the professional risk manager and it's not just for huge corporations. It's a versatile management tool that can, and should, be used by everyone.

"The most elegant forms of managerial decision involve problems that never have to be solved because they are prevented from occurring... they are anticipated and side-stepped. The deliberate non-catastrophe is one of the most effective contributions a manager can make."

James Martin, author

The appendices contain a list of potential risks and possible countermeasures, an example risk register and some additional sources of information.

Examples of risks and possible countermeasures

The following tables show some examples of risks within the various categories introduced in Chapter 2, along with some of the possible countermeasures for each. Although the risks shown here have been assigned to the categories that seemed most obvious to the author at the time of writing, there are no hard and fast rules and you may choose to categorise them differently for the purposes of your risk assessment within your own business (e.g. operator error appears in the "Operational – production and distribution" category but may equally be shown under "Personnel").

Please note that the examples are provided as a guide only. The risks and/or countermeasures shown may or may not be applicable to your business. If in any doubt you should seek expert advice.

Risk	Possible countermeasure(s)
Strategic: Failure to achieve strategic objectives (e.g. sales, growth, new markets/ products/ services, etc.)	• Strategic planning; • Investment; • Competitor analysis; • SWOT analysis; • Innovation; • Effective leadership and direction; • Staff and management objectives aligned with strategic objectives; • Awareness.
Operational – premises: Fire	• Smoke/heat detectors/alarms; • Fire alarm/link to fire station; • Automatic fire suppression system; • Fire extinguishers; • Staff training/awareness; • Safe/secure storage of flammable materials; • Security; • Power off equipment when not in use; • Insurance; • Contingency plan.
Flood (natural)	• Location – check surrounding area/ flood history before taking on premises; • Check for adequate drainage/blockages; • Insurance; • Contingency plan.

Risk	Possible countermeasure(s)
Operational – premises (continued):	
Flood (water leak)	• Equipment location (e.g. not below water tanks/kitchen/bathroom/etc. or in basement); • Check for presence of pipework above (e.g. central heating boilers); • Drainage channels/water detectors; • Maintenance; • Contingency plan.
Explosion	• Proper storage of explosive materials; • Security (anti-terrorist/activist measures); • Understand risks posed by neighbouring businesses; • Contingency plan.
Building damage (e.g. storm damage)	• Building maintenance; • Lightning protection; • Contingency plan.
Denial of access	• Understand risks posed by neighbouring businesses (e.g. fire, explosion, malicious damage); • Contingency plan.
Break-in/theft/vandalism	• Security guards/patrols; • CCTV; • Intruder alarms; • Access control; • Safe; • Don't keep valuables on site; • Insurance.

Risk	Possible countermeasure(s)
Operational – premises (continued):	
Power outage	• Uninterruptible power supplies (UPS); • Generator (fixed or via "ship-in" contract); • Dual feeds/diverse cable routes; • Contingency plan.
Operational – production and distribution:	
Supply problems (e.g. components or raw materials)	• Multiple/alternative suppliers; • Stock control; • Forecasting; • Buffer stocks; • Contract terms and conditions (e.g. penalty clauses).
Insufficient capacity	• Forecasting; • Outsourcing; • Additional shifts; • Temporary staff.
Plant/equipment failure	See "Technology – plant and equipment" on page 119.
Transport/distribution problems	• Vehicle maintenance; • Outsourcing; • Contingency plan.
Fuel shortage	• Forward planning; • Own fuel supplies; • Efficient route planning; • Delay non-critical deliveries; • Customer liaison.

Risk	Possible countermeasure(s)
Operational – production and distribution (continued):	
Operator errors	• Training; • Processes and procedures; • Documentation; • Supervision; • Monitoring and reporting; • Quality control.
Pollution/contamination/ environmental damage	• Training; • Processes and procedures; • Documentation; • Supervision; • Monitoring and reporting; • Quality control; • Outsourcing of high risk processes; • Use less dangerous/more environmentally friendly products; • Contingency plan.
Inadequate skills/skills shortage	See "Personnel" on page 116.
Industrial action	See "Personnel" on page 116.
Financial/Commercial:	
Cash flow problems	• Payment terms; • Prompt invoicing; • Credit control; • Stock control; • Overdraft; • Factoring;

Risk	Possible countermeasure(s)
Financial/Commercial (continued):	
Cash flow problems (continued)	• Forecasting; • Avoid over commitment; • Address problems early (e.g. talk to customers/bank).
Insufficient sales	• Sales pipeline; • Business plan.
Inadequate profits	• Pricing strategy; • Cost control; • Accurate management information (e.g. costs).
Loss of customers/major customer	• Customer satisfaction surveys; • Contract reviews; • Account management; • Limit % business from any one customer (avoid "all eggs in one basket").
Breach of contract	• Understand contract terms and conditions; • Professional indemnity insurance.
Interest rates increase	• Fixed rate loans; • Hedging.
Exchange rate fluctuations	• Sterling payments; • Payment terms; • Hedging.

Risk	Possible countermeasure(s)
Financial/Commercial (continued):	
Changes in consumer behaviour	• Market intelligence; • Marketing plan; • New products or services.
Regulatory/compliance:	

Breach of regulation
Failure to meet legal/
contractual requirements
Loss of operating licence
	• Keep abreast of applicable
	  regulations/legislation;
	• Training;
	• Awareness;
	• Senior-level responsibility for
	  compliance.

Litigation	• Above plus insurance.
Health and safety:	
Accidental injury or death	• Policies and procedures; • Training and awareness; • Health and safety risk assessments; • Insurance.
Litigation	• Insurance.
Personnel:	
Loss or unavailability of key staff	• Insurance ("key man"/sickness/life); • Succession planning; • Cross-training; • Document key processes; • Job rotation; • Contract/agency staff.

Risk	Possible countermeasure(s)
Personnel (continued):	
Inadequate skills/skills shortage	• Skills matrix; • Forward planning; • Training; • Recruitment; • Contract/agency staff; • Automation; • Outsourcing.
Inability to recruit suitable staff	• Review selection criteria vs. remuneration; • Review candidate sources (e.g. agencies used, headhunting, advertising, etc.); • Use of contract staff.
Industrial action	• Good staff relations.
Workplace violence/bullying	• Policies and procedures (e.g. disciplinary); • Clear guidelines; • Communication; • Monitoring/management.
Claims from employees/customers (e.g. public liability, negligence)	• Insurance (e.g. Employers' and Public Liability); • Health and Safety risk assessments; • Policies and procedures.

Risk	Possible countermeasure(s)
Technology – **IT and telecommunications:**	
Hardware problems	• Support/maintenance contract; • Duplicate/redundant equipment; • Backups; • Recovery plans; • Spare equipment; • Replacement equipment contract.
Software problems (operating system and applications)	• Legal software; • Don't load non-essential software; • Support contract; • Schedule of regular upgrades.
Telephony failure	• Dual feed into the building; • Diverse routing of cables (separate access routes, separate exchanges); • Switchboard – see hardware and software problems (above).
Unavailability of support staff	• Long notice periods for key staff; • Regular staff reviews; • Cross-training; • Succession planning.
External data communications failure	• Dual feed/diverse routing; • Multiple service providers.

Risk	Possible countermeasure(s)
Technology – IT and telecommunications (continued):	
Virus	• Virus protection – files; • Virus protection – e-mails; • Regular anti-virus software updates.
Hacker/unauthorised access	• "Good" passwords; • Force regular password changes; • Information security policy; • Firewall; • Ensure all staff logoff when finished; • Clear desk policy and secure storage for paper-based records.
Sabotage/malicious damage	• Leavers' passwords reset, keys, etc. returned; • "Garden leave" where appropriate; • Confidentiality agreements; • Restrict access to sensitive/personal data; • IT security policy.
Data loss	• Backups; • Information security policy.
Data integrity compromised	• Data entry integrity checks/controls.

Risk	Possible countermeasure(s)
Technology – plant and equipment:	
Plant/equipment failure	• Maintenance; • Duplicate/redundant/spare equipment; • Outsourcing; • Contingency plans.
Obsolescence	• Planning; • Investment.
Projects:	
Failure to meet timescales Increased cost/resource requirements Business requirements not met Project failure	• Effective project management; • Skilled/experienced project manager(s); • Clear understanding of business requirements; • Formal project management methodology (including risk assessment); • Training.
Miscellaneous:	
Loss of paper-based/ desktop-based/archived information	• Identify all vital records; • Offsite copies of vital/important records; • Adequate, secure storage for "live" documents; • Archive infrequently accessed data; • Document control policy.

Example risk register

#	Risk	Likelihood	Impact	Rating	Opportunity	Countermeasures	In place?	Actions/status/ comments	Person responsible	Due date/ complete

Department/business function:

Completed by:

Date :

Likelihood (1-4)
Impact (1-4)
Risk rating (Px1)

Y or N
or rating
(e.g. none, low, medium, high)

BS31100 Risk Management Code of Practice – British Standards Institution, ISBN 978-0-580-57434-4.

The Complete Guide to Business Risk Management (second edition) – Kit Sadgrove (Gower Publishing), ISBN 978-0-566-08661-8.

Five Steps to Risk Assessment (leaflet) – Health and Safety Executive (HSE Books), ISBN 0-7176-6189-X.

Practical Business Continuity Management – Andy Osborne (Word4Word), ISBN 978-1-906316-01-3.

Risk Management – Institute of Directors (Director Publications), ISBN 1-9045-2044-8.

The Gist of Process Mapping: how to record, analyse and improve work processes – Alan C. Clark (Word4Word), ISBN 0-9541209-9-X.

A Risk Management Standard (AIRMIC, ALARM, IRM) – downloadable from any of the associations' websites.

Some useful sources of information

Acumen Business Services Ltd.
www.acumen-bcp.co.uk
PO Box 92, Evesham, Worcestershire, WR11 7FN
Telephone: 01386 834455

Association of Insurance and Risk Managers (AIRMIC)
www.airmic.com
6 Lloyd's Avenue, London, EC3N 3AX
Telephone: 020 7480 7610

ALARM (public sector risk management association)
www.alarm-uk.com
Ladysmith House, High Street, Sidmouth, EX10 8LN
Telephone: 01395 519083

Business Link
www.businesslink.gov.uk
Helpline: 0845 600 9006

Business Continuity Institute
www.thebci.org
10 Southview Park, Marsack Street, Caversham, RG4 5AF
Telephone: 0118 947 8215

Continuity, Insurance and Risk (CIR)
www.cirmagazine.com

Dependency.com (dependency modelling)
www.dependency.com

Directgov ("How businesses can prepare for emergencies" page)

www.direct.gov.uk/en/Governmentcitizensandrights/Dealingwithemergencies/
Preparingforemergencies/DG_176539

Environment Agency (UK)

www.environment-agency.gov.uk

National Customer Contact Centre, PO Box 544, Rotherham, S60 1BY

Enquiries: 0870 850 6506

Floodline: 0845 988 1188

Incident hotline: 0800 807 060

Fire Protection Association

www.thefpa.co.uk

London Road, Moreton-in-Marsh, Gloucestershire, GL56 0RH

Telephone: 01608 812500

Health & Safety Executive

www.hse.gov.uk

(IG) Redgrave Court, Merton Road, Bootle, Merseyside L20 7HS

Infoline: 0845 345 0055

Publications: 01787 881165

Institute of Risk Management (IRM)

www.theirm.org

6 Lloyd's Avenue, London, EC3N 3AX

Telephone: 020 7709 9808

Local Resilience Forums

http://www.cabinetoffice.gov.uk/ukresilience/preparedness/ukgovernment/lrfs.aspx

(contact details for Local Resilience Forums throughout England and Wales).

National Security Inspectorate

www.nsi.org.uk

Sentinel House, 5 Reform Road, Maidenhead, SL6 8BY

Telephone: 01628 637512

UK Resilience

www.ukresilience.info

Cabinet Office, 22 Whitehall, London, SW1A 2WH

Telephone: 020 7276 1234

http://www.cabinetoffice.gov.uk/ukresilience/preparedness/ukgovernment/lrfs.aspx

NB: The above information is provided for reference and educational purposes only and should not be considered as an endorsement of any company, organisation, product or service. All details were correct at the time of going to press.

Acknowledgements and thanks

"Risk Response Options" section and final paragraph in "Me, a risk manager" section based on original text by Ian Charters, first published in chapter 9 of **The Definitive Guide to Business Continuity Management**, Wiley, 1999.

Diagram in "Addressing our risks" section based on an original by James Royds of SRM.

Elements of "Setting the corporate risk appetite" inspired by a suggested approach presented by John Robinson of Inoni.

Elements of the roles and responsibilities shown in "A culture of risk awareness" based on original text in section 6 of **A Risk Management Standard**, published in 2002 by AIRMIC, ALARM and IRM.

A big thank you goes to the following people, who kindly took the time to review and comment on the draft manuscript and/or share their thoughts on risk management: Rosie Bhattacharjee, Ian Charters, Tom Dawn, Jagdeep Gogna, Richard Kennedy, Andy Marshall, Beverley Osborne (proofreader extraordinaire!), Peter Taylor, Richard Ward and Robert Whitehouse. Chris Baker for providing information on dependency modelling and, Richard Ward for writing the foreword.